NEW VANGUARD • 155

BRITISH AIRSHIPS 1905–30

IAN CASTLE ILLUSTRATED BY TONY BRYAN & GIUSEP

First published in Great Britain in 2009 by Osprey Publishing,
Midland House, West Way, Botley, Oxford, OX2 0PH, UK

443 Park Avenue South, New York, NY 10016, USA

E-mail: info@ospreypublishing.com

A CIP catalogue record for this book is available from the British Library

Print ISBN: 978 1 84603 387 2

PDF e-book ISBN: 978 184603 895 2

Page layout by: Melissa Orrom Swan, Oxford

Index by Alan Thatcher

Typeset in Sabon and Myriad Pro

Originated by PDQ Digital Media Solutions Ltd.

Printed in China through Worldprint Ltd.

09 10 11 12 13   10 9 8 7 6 5 4 3 2 1

FOR A CATALOGUE OF ALL BOOKS PUBLISHED BY OSPREY MILITARY AND
AVIATION PLEASE CONTACT:

NORTH AMERICA

Osprey Direct, c/o Random House Distribution Center, 400 Hahn Road,
Westminster, MD 21157

E-mail: uscustomerservice@ospreypublishing.com

ALL OTHER REGIONS

Osprey Direct, The Book Service Ltd, Distribution Centre, Colchester Road,
Frating Green, Colchester, Essex, CO7 7DW

E-mail: customerservice@ospreypublishing.com

Osprey Publishing is supporting the Woodland Trust, the UK's leading
woodland conservation charity, by funding the dedication of trees.

www.ospreypublishing.com

ACKNOWLEDGEMENTS

The dream of powered lighter-than-air flight fascinated man for centuries,
yet it was only the enlightened minds of French and German engineers
and designers that made it practical towards the end of the 19th century.
It is a fascinating journey from these early beginnings to the vast globe-
crossing leviathans that took to the skies just a few decades later. The
journey to condense Britain's varied and innovative contribution to this
sphere of aeronautics into this volume has at times proved testing, but
it is one I have enjoyed immensely. The book would not have taken its
present form without the information I have been able to draw from
the National Archives at Kew, the Imperial War Museum in Lambeth,
the Airship Heritage Trust and the Royal Air Force Museum at Hendon.
I would particularly like to thank Andrew Simpson, Curator, Department
of Aircraft and Exhibits, at the RAF Museum who supplied me with much
information on airship R.33 and unhesitatingly answered my questions
on the minutiae of aeroplane design.

Unless otherwise stated, all illustrations are from my own collection.

DEDICATION

For Nicola

CONTENTS

INTRODUCTION   4

AIRSHIP TYPES   5

ARMY AIRSHIP ORGANISATION   5

THE ARMY AIRSHIPS   6

EARLY NAVY AIRSHIPS   12

EARLY WAR SERVICE   15

NAVAL AIRSHIPS 1914–18   16

SEMI-RIGID (SR) AIRSHIPS   25

RIGID AIRSHIPS   26

BRITISH AIRSHIPS AT WAR   38

SUMMARY   44

SELECT BIBLIOGRAPHY   47

INDEX   48

BRITISH AIRSHIPS 1905–30

INTRODUCTION

The *Willows I*. This, the first of E. T. Willows's six airship designs, experienced problems with weight distribution, causing the envelope to sag in the middle. By fitting a longer-framework car, the problem was overcome and the airship attracted keen interest from Col J. E. Capper, commander of the Royal Engineers Balloon School.

At the end of the 19th century, when the other great powers, Germany and France, were enthusiastically embracing the development and construction of lighter-than-air aircraft – airships – Britain officially showed little interest in the evolving science. The first airship to achieve a successful flight in Britain was built and piloted by Stanley Spencer, a balloon-maker and aeronaut. Taking off from Crystal Palace, South London, in 1902, Spencer flew towards the City, but, with his 3hp engine unable to make progress against the wind, he turned west and eventually landed at Eastcote near Ruislip. Spencer continued building airships but it was one designed and flown by Ernest Thompson Willows, a 19-year-old Welshman, in 1905 that attracted more serious attention. His *Willows No.1*, powered by a 7hp Peugeot motorcycle engine, was the first in a series of six airships eventually built by Willows. Importantly, it gained the attention of the War Office and in 1907, under the direction of brevet Col J. E. Capper, commander of the Royal Engineers Balloon School, the Army began to build its own airship.

AIRSHIP TYPES

There are three types of airship: rigid, semi-rigid and non-rigid. All are classed as dirigibles – steerable balloons.

On 5 October 1907 *Nulli Secundus* flew over London, but strong headwinds on the return journey forced it to land at Crystal Palace, having been in the air for 3 hours 25 minutes.

The rigid airship is the type exemplified by the German Zeppelins. This type is formed of a lightweight rigid framework of metal or wood from which cars (or gondolas) containing the controls and engines are suspended. Within this framework are a number of individual large cells containing the lifting gas, highly inflammable hydrogen. An outer skin, known as the envelope, covered the framework; it is the framework that gives the rigid airship its shape.

In semi-rigid airships the envelope maintains its shape by the pressure of the gas inside and the use of an external keel running the length of the ship which supports the car and adds rigidity.

The third type – the non-rigid – was that most favoured and exploited by Britain during World War I. As the name suggests, the envelope retains its shape through gas pressure, but when an airship ascends the gas expands, and when it descends again the gas contracts, so without internal air compartments, or ballonets, the envelope would lose shape and become unmanageable. Air collected from the propeller slipstream, distributed via an air duct through non-return valves, increased pressure in the ballonets, allowing the envelope to retain its shape. It is the non-rigid type of airship that is often called a 'blimp'.

The basic principle of any airship was by the use of hydrogen, a lighter-than-air gas, to produce lift greater than the total fixed weight of the airship itself. This excess lift, known as the disposable or useful lift, determined the weight of crew, fuel, ballast, weapons and stores that could be carried.

ARMY AIRSHIP ORGANISATION

The Army's first involvement in lighter-than-air experiments began with the establishment by the Royal Engineers of the Army Balloon Equipment Store at Woolwich in 1878. By 1890 the unit expanded into the Balloon Section, with a factory and school at Chatham, relocating to Aldershot in 1902. Three years later the Balloon Section moved the short distance to Farnborough and in 1909 the Balloon Factory transferred to civilian control. Then, in April 1911, the Balloon School became the Air Battalion (No.1 Coy Airships;

The rebuilt version of Capper's airship, *Nulli Secundus II*, had a short life. First flown in July 1908, it was scrapped at the end of the following month.

No.2 Coy Aeroplanes) of the Royal Engineers while the Balloon Factory became the Army Aircraft Factory (later, the Royal Aircraft Factory). However, the following year the Air Battalion formed the basis of the military wing of the fledgling Royal Flying Corps.

THE ARMY AIRSHIPS

Nulli Secundus and *Nulli Secundus II*

Col Capper received approval to begin construction of a government-funded airship in 1907. Together with the Chief Kiting Officer, S. F. Cody, he designed and built *Nulli Secundus* ('Second to none'). Its 110ft cylindrical envelope, constructed of goldbeater's skin, held 55,000 cubic feet (cu.ft) of hydrogen. Goldbeater's skin is an extraordinary material, being both lightweight and gas-tight, and made from the intestines of cattle. *Nulli Secundus* used some 200,000 skins, fixed, 15 layers thick, to a cloth backing and varnished. Below the envelope a triangular steel framework hung, attached by a net and four broad silk bands. A small car suspended below the framework held the 50hp Antoinette engine driving two propellers. The framework carried a rudder and elevators at the rear and two moveable horizontal elevators at the front. The first test flight of *Nulli Secundus* took place in September 1907 and then, on 5 October, with Capper and Cody on board, it flew from Farnborough to London, becoming the first airship to appear over the capital.

Capper carried out a number of alterations and launched the paradoxically named *Nulli Secundus II* in July 1908 as a semi-rigid. Small changes to the envelope gave a capacity of 56,000cu.ft and a new-style open car was added to the framework, now covered with waterproofed silk and attached directly to the envelope. A number of unconvincing short flights took place before the airship was dismantled at the end of August 1908.

Baby, *Beta* and *Beta II*

Capper continued with his experimental work and in May 1909 he revealed his new craft. Smaller than his two previous models, this non-rigid had an envelope of 84ft with a diameter of 24ft and a hydrogen capacity of 21,000cu.ft, containing one ballonet. Its small size earned it the name *Baby*.

The second version of Capper's small airship *Baby*. It differed in shape to *Nulli Secundus*, being described by those who saw it for the first time as a 'huge sunfish'. When Capper finished his experiments with it he commented that it had 'given assistance in solving various problems'.

The goldbeater's skin envelope had two inflated horizontal fins at the stern with a canvas sail fin on the underside. An inflated upper fin later replaced the underside sail. The car, initially of an open framework, was later covered with canvas and carried two 8hp Buchet engines, each driving a single propeller. These were later replaced by a single, more powerful 20–25hp REP motor driving both propellers, attaining a speed of about 20mph. *Baby* flew for the last time in December 1909, when Capper prepared to reconstruct it.

Baby was reborn as *Beta* in May 1910, with an enlarged envelope capacity of 35,000cu.ft and an overall length of 104ft. To aid stability, the former inflatable rear fins were replaced with fixed planes, two horizontal and one vertical on the underside, to which a rudder was attached. The car was again of a long open framework, with elevators fixed to the front, and held a 35hp Green engine powering two propellers with space for a three-man crew in the centre. *Beta* proved to be a generally reliable craft although it experienced many problems with its fragile envelope.

Beta became the focus of numerous experiments during its life, including the first wireless message transmitted from an airship and the first instance of a non-rigid airship being attached to a mooring mast.

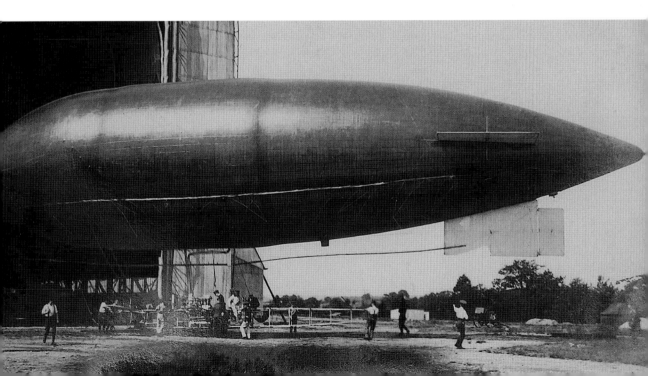

The redesigned car of *Beta II* was boat-shaped with seats for a three-man crew. The car is on display in the Aviation Hall of the Science Museum, London.

Late in 1912 a redesigned *Beta* reappeared as *Beta II*. With a larger goldbeater's skin envelope of 50,000cu.ft and a 45hp Clerget engine added in a new car, it achieved a maximum speed of 35mph. The forward elevators on the first *Beta* had lacked efficiency; they were replaced by attaching moveable surfaces to the rear horizontal planes. In 1913 *Beta II* took part in army exercises and was used extensively for training purposes.

Gamma and *Gamma II*

The first version of *Gamma* at Farnborough, showing one of the inflated rear fins, the fixed lower plane with rudder and the open-framework car.

In February 1910 Capper launched his latest airship, the *Gamma*, which carried a crew of four. It was the first British airship to utilize an envelope made of rubberized cotton fabric, manufactured by the Astra Company of Paris. The initial envelope on this non-rigid was 154ft in length with a capacity of 75,000cu.ft and it bore two horizontal inflated stabilizing fins

and a single fixed plane vertically below. The open-framework car, made of steel and hickory, carried the 80hp Green engine and had two pairs of elevators attached, one pair forward and the other to the rear. The engine drove a pair of swivelling propellers, pioneered by Willows, designed to increase manoeuvrability.

By June 1910 *Gamma* had a new car fitted with shorter framework, 21ft long and 6ft wide; the forward and aft elevators were replaced with a box-kite tail plane, and the inflated fins with fixed types. In addition, two 45hp Iris engines superseded the Green, each driving a single propeller. Following these changes, and with a new envelope of 101,000cu.ft fitted in 1912, it became known as *Gamma II*, able to carry six people – crew and passengers (although nine were carried at the 1912 army manoeuvres) – as well as wireless equipment and enough fuel for an eight-hour journey.

Gamma II with its 101,000cu.ft envelope, box-kite tail plane and fixed stabilizing fins. When the twin Iris engines were fitted it was found necessary for the mechanic to sit on a platform between them to control lubrication. Maj Bannerman, commander of the Air Battalion, commented: 'His position will not be an enviable one.'

Foreign imports: *Clément-Bayard II* and *Lebaudy Morning Post*

Any reader of the British press in the early years of the 20th century could not fail to be aware of the dramatic progress made by the Zeppelin airships in Germany. When this was compared with the British Army's experimental work, it was clear that Britain lagged a long way behind Germany, and France too. Pressure mounted on the government and in October 1910 the *Clément-Bayard II* arrived in Britain from France, a non-rigid airship that 'could be examined, tested, and, if approved of, purchased for the nation'. The ship's envelope was 251ft long with a capacity of 247,000cu.ft; two 120hp Clément-Bayard engines supplied the power.

After initial disagreement over the price, the airship was eventually purchased for £18,000 – before completing its prescribed tests. In addition, the *Daily Mail* newspaper paid for a shed to be erected on Wormwood Scrubs in London in which to house it.

Another newspaper, the *Morning Post*, raised £18,000 from its readers to purchase a Lebaudy airship from France and presented it to the government. Known as the *Lebaudy Morning Post*, the new airship arrived ten days after the *Clément-Bayard II*. It was a semi-rigid with an envelope of 337ft and a

gas capacity of 353,000cu.ft. Disaster struck almost immediately. As handlers guided it into the new shed at Farnborough, specially built to house it, a girder in the roof caught the envelope and ripped it open – the manufacturers had increased its height without informing Farnborough. It was not until May the following year that the *Morning Post* was ready to fly again, but a fresh disaster struck which saw it wrecked on Farnborough Common. After this second incident the *Morning Post* was scrapped.

Delta

In 1910 design work commenced on *Delta*, the next Army airship, a semi-rigid with a waterproofed silk envelope. Construction work began the following year on what proved to be a troubled development. The envelope proved a failure as it burst when under full gas pressure; a new envelope of rubberized fabric, 225ft long with a capacity of 160,000cu.ft, replaced it. Experiments to attach girders to the envelope to bear the weight of the car failed, leading to the redesign of *Delta* as a non-rigid, and it finally took to the air in September 1912. It had a 26ft open car fitted with two 110hp White & Poppe engines driving twin swivelling propellers that attained a speed of 44mph. However, with problems continuing to dog it, *Delta* did not enter service until October 1913. A later refit appears to have added a larger envelope of about 175,000cu.ft.

Eta

Eta was the Army's last experimental airship. With an envelope capacity of 118,000cu.ft, *Eta* was smaller than *Delta* when it took to the air for the first time in August 1913. Initially it encountered a number of mechanical problems but when these were rectified it became an efficient ship. The rubberized fabric envelope contained two ballonets and was fitted with horizontal side planes with elevators and a vertical lower plane carrying the rudder. The most important innovation on *Eta* was the suspension system securing the car to the envelope. The six rigging wires from the car each divided into two, then each of these branches divided again into three close to the envelope, where the 36 individual wires were attached to 'D' rings fixed to fan-shaped patches stuck to the envelope with adhesive and then sewn into place. These became known as 'Eta patches' and became a common feature on subsequent non-rigid airships.

However, on 1 January 1914, following a government decision, responsibility for all airship development passed from the Army to the Navy (leading to the cancellation of the Army's next airships, *Epsilon I* and *II*) and at that point the Army's existing airships, *Beta II*, *Gamma II*, *Delta* and *Eta*, transferred to naval control.

After a long development *Delta* proved a useful craft. Between 27 July and 31 December 1913 it made 53 ascents, flying a total of 2,035 miles. Also in 1913, Maj E. M. Maitland, RE, used *Delta* to make the first parachute jump from n airship.

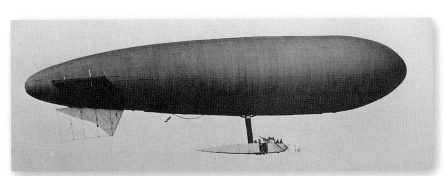

The tapering car on the *Eta*, built on a steel framework, was a development of the *Gamma* car and carried a crew of five, two in front of the pair of 80hp Canton-Unné engines driving the swivelling propellers, and three behind.

EARLY NAVY AIRSHIPS

Rigid Naval Airship No.1

The Navy's early involvement in airship development lagged significantly behind the Army; however, in 1908 the government announced that it wished to explore the threat posed to Britain by airships, deciding that the best way to analyse this threat was to build one and test its capabilities. The Admiralty therefore detailed a team to work with Vickers Sons & Maxim Ltd to design and develop a rigid airship. Construction began at Barrow-in-Furness in 1909.

The airship, officially named *Rigid Naval Airship No.1*, earned the popular name of *Mayfly* and first emerged from its shed on 22 May 1911. The vast envelope extended for 512ft, built on a duralumin framework; Zeppelins were not built of this extremely light but strong aluminium alloy until late 1914. The envelope covered 17 individual gas-bags, which held 663,518cu.ft of hydrogen. Two Wolseley 180hp engines, each mounted in a watertight wooden gondola, supplied the power; the forward engine drove two four-bladed propellers while the rear engine powered a larger single propeller.

A number of tests took place over the next few days before the airship returned to its shed. Exactly four months passed before, fatefully, it emerged again, on 24 September 1911. Caught by a powerful gust of wind, it became unstable. Then, disastrously, it broke in two. It was deemed beyond repair, and the whole project was scrapped and the Admiralty's involvement in airship development ceased for a while.

Pre-war naval airships

In 1912 renewed concerns over German airship development caused the Navy to refocus its attention. Turning to the civilian airship designer E. T. Willows, the Navy purchased *Willows No.4* for training purposes (renaming it His Majesty's Airship [HMA] No.2) and then, with no others available in Britain, looked overseas, purchasing an Astra-Torres airship from France and a Parseval from Germany 'for training and experimental purposes'. Attempts to purchase a Zeppelin failed as the German government banned their sale to foreign powers. In addition the Navy ordered an Italian Forlanini with an option for two more, but the deal never materialised because of the onset of World War I.

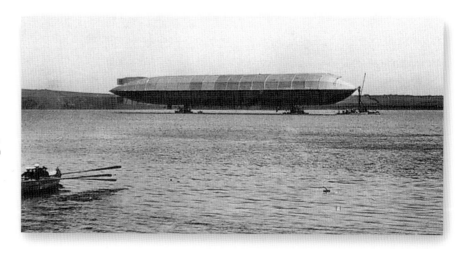

The first outing of *Mayfly*. With its gas-bags fully inflated, it was hauled across Cavendish Dock, Barrow-in-Furness, and attached to a mooring mast, where it remained for almost four days, successfully withstanding gusts of wind up to 45mph.

Foreign imports: Astra-Torres and Parseval

The Astra-Torres (HMA No.3) made its first flight from Farnborough on 12 June 1913. The shape of the envelope, which had a great influence on later British airship design, was strikingly different from anything previously seen in Britain, being formed of three lobes, two at the bottom and one on top, connected by internal porous fabric curtains. The envelope was 248ft long and its capacity was around 230,000cu.ft. Two 200hp Chenu engines supplied the power to drive the pair of two-bladed propellers mounted high above the solid-looking enclosed gondola. The Astra-Torres achieved a speed of 51mph in trials, with ascent and descent controlled by moving the entire gondola forward or back, by power or manually. A single fin, positioned vertically under the stern, carried fixed stabilizing planes. This arrangement proved unsatisfactory and a new vertical fin with improved rudder and horizontal fins with elevators replaced it.

The Parseval (HMA No.4), built by the Parseval Airship Company in Germany, arrived in May 1913 but did not make its first flight until 30 June 1913. The trial flights were successful and in August the Navy confirmed its option on three more. However, the onset of the war prevented delivery. Instead Vickers, who had earlier agreed a deal with Parseval to build airships to their design under licence, undertook the work.

HMA No.2 (*Willows IV*) with *Beta* in the background. HMA No.2 was purchased by the Admiralty in July 1912 as a training ship, but later its envelope was attached to a BE2c aeroplane fuselage and became the prototype of the SS Class.

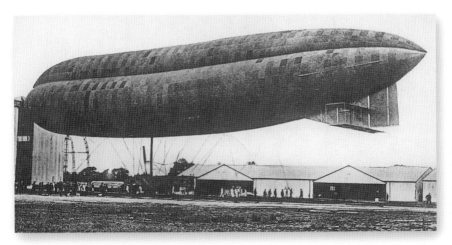

The success in trials of the non-rigid Astra-Torres (HMA No.3), shown here, led to the order of three more of these airships. The first of them (HMA No.8) was delivered in 1914 but it appears unlikely that the other two (HMA No.10 and HMA No.16) ever saw service.

The streamlined outline of the Parseval design (HMA No.4) is clearly shown here. The open car, seating a crew of seven, carried two 180hp Maybach engines capable of a top speed of 43mph.

The Parseval, a non-rigid airship, had a streamlined envelope tapering to a fine point at the stern, with an overall capacity of 310,640cu.ft and a length of 275ft – although by February 1914 the length had been increased to 312ft, giving an increased capacity of 364,000cu.ft. The envelope contained two ballonets that could be used to adjust trim, as could hauling the gondola forward or aft through a system of pulleys. This first Parseval was not fitted with elevators on the rear fins, but this changed after the initial trials. A precarious machine-gun position was located on top of the envelope with access via a tube connected to the gondola. The later models produced by Vickers (HMA Nos.5, 6 and 7), appearing in the latter part of 1917, all had the larger envelope. No.5, which served as a training ship for crews of rigids, had a large covered gondola with fixed propellers driven by two 240hp Renault engines fitted at either end of the car. Nos. 6 and 7 were identical to each other, having enclosed cars of a smaller design than No.5, carrying twin 180hp engines driving swivelling propellers mounted on either side of the car.

New designations

On 1 January 1914, when all Army airships transferred to the naval wing of the Royal Flying Corps, they received new designations within the Navy numbering system, listing airships in a sequence based on the placing of

One of the Parsevals built by Vickers, HMA No.7, about to make its first trial flight on 22 December 1917. It was identical to HMA No.6 and, after its trial, was relegated to providing spares for its sister airship.

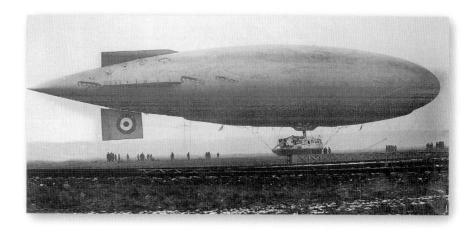

production orders. By the time the war began, the naval wing had left the Royal Flying Corps and formed the Royal Naval Air Service (RNAS).

HMA No.1r	Mayfly (rigid – dismantled)
HMA No.2	*Willows No.4*
HMA No.3	Astra-Torres
HMA No.4	Parseval
HMA No.5	Vickers Parseval
HMA No.6	Vickers Parseval
HMA No.7	Vickers Parseval
HMA No.8	Astra-Torres
HMA No.9r	Vickers (rigid)
HMA No.10	Astra-Torres
HMA No.11	Forlanini (undelivered)
HMA No.12	Forlanini (undelivered)
HMA No.13	Forlanini (undelivered)
HMA No.14r	Armstrong Whitworth (rigid – cancelled)
HMA No.15r	Armstrong Whitworth (rigid – cancelled)
HMA No.16	Astra-Torres
HMA No.17	*Beta II* (ex-Army)
HMA No.18	*Gamma II* (ex-Army)
HMA No.19	*Delta* (ex-Army)
HMA No.20	*Eta* (ex-Army)
HMA No.21	*Epsilon I* (ex-Army – cancelled)
HMA No.22	*Epsilon II* (ex-Army – cancelled)

However, at the outbreak of World War I the only serviceable airships were HMA No.2 (*Willows IV*) for training, No.3 (Astra-Torres), No.4 (Parseval) and the four former Army vessels, No.17 (*Beta II*), No.18 (*Gamma II*), No.19 (*Delta*) and No.20 (*Eta*).

EARLY WAR SERVICE

The day after the declaration of war, HMA No.4, ironically the German-built Parseval, performed an overnight patrol along the Thames estuary and over the North Sea looking for approaching German warships. On its return the following morning it came under rifle fire from soldiers of a Territorial division who believed it was a German airship, but fortunately it suffered

In response to the Admiralty's demand for an easily produced airship to search for U-boats in Britain's coastal waters, the RNAS team at Kingsnorth developed, built and received approval for the Submarine Scout, based on a BE2c aircraft fuselage, in just three weeks. (Imperial War Museum Q.68276)

no damage. Both No.4 and No.3, the Astra-Torres, patrolled the English Channel to protect the British Expeditionary Force as it sailed across to France and continued patrols in the area for some time afterwards. No.3 also accompanied an RNAS detachment sent to Ostend. Later, when back in England, No.3, along with No.17 (*Beta II*) and No.20 (*Eta*) flew night-time reconnaissance over London in September 1914 to evaluate the potential threat posed by raiding Zeppelins. Then, in November, while flying to Dunkirk to join another RNAS detachment, No.20 (*Eta*) ran into a snowstorm near Redhill in Surrey, suffering considerable damage. An inspection declared it beyond repair. No.17 (*Beta II*), sent to France to replace *Eta*, flew a number of reconnaissance missions and carried out a spotting mission for the Belgian artillery before returning in February 1915 to operate as a training airship. No.18 (*Gamma II*) became a focus for mooring experiments while No.19 (*Delta*) did not serve because of a damaged gondola. HMA No.8, one of the second batch of Astra-Torres airships, delivered to the RNAS in December 1914, carried out a number of patrols in the eastern approaches to the English Channel during 1915.

NAVAL AIRSHIPS 1914–18

Submarine Scout (SS) Class

With the land war settling into the stalemate of trench warfare, Germany turned to its submarine fleet to take the war to Britain, attempting to cut its vital seaborne trade routes. The U-boats began to exact a heavy toll on British shipping and, to counter this, the Admiralty called a meeting on 28 February 1915 attended by representatives of the RNAS and two private firms, Airships

A **THE SUBMARINE SCOUTS**

Developed by a team at RNAS Kingsnorth, the design of the Submarine Scout amalgamated existing technology using the 35,000cu.ft envelope from HMA No.2, the suspension patches originally devised for the *Eta* and a BE2c aeroplane fuselage, minus its wings and tail arrangements. When it went into production a larger 60,000cu.ft envelope was fitted. The result was a hybrid **(1)**, but it worked.

A second type of SS airship followed, using a Maurice Farman type fuselage with a rear-fitted 'pusher' propeller **(2)**. The suspension arrangements were similar to those on the BE2c although it could be fitted either to a 60,000 or a 70,000cu.ft envelope.

A third type **(3)**, based on the Armstrong Whitworth FK.3 aeroplane, finally appeared in 1916 after the prototype had received approval in July 1915. This type used a 70,000cu.ft envelope.

SS.1, SS.3–SS.26, SS.48–SS.49	BE2c type
SS.2	Airships Ltd prototype
SS.27, SS.39A*–SS.47	Armstrong Whitworth type
SS.28–SS.39*	Maurice Farman type

*SS.39 was originally built with a Maurice Farman fuselage but wrecked in July 1917. It was reconstructed as SS.39A with an Armstrong Whitworth fuselage.

After meeting the Admiralty's initial requirements, the Submarine Scouts evolved and improved through the 'Pusher', 'Zero' and 'Twin' variants. But it was the Zero **(4)** that made the biggest impact, with a total of 77 being built. One pilot, T. B. Williams, considered that the Zeros were 'dreams come true' and described his as 'my beautiful airship'. Recounting his experiences, Williams admitted that he would 'shout and slap the flanks of the control car when we were charging into battle, much to the amusement of my crew'.

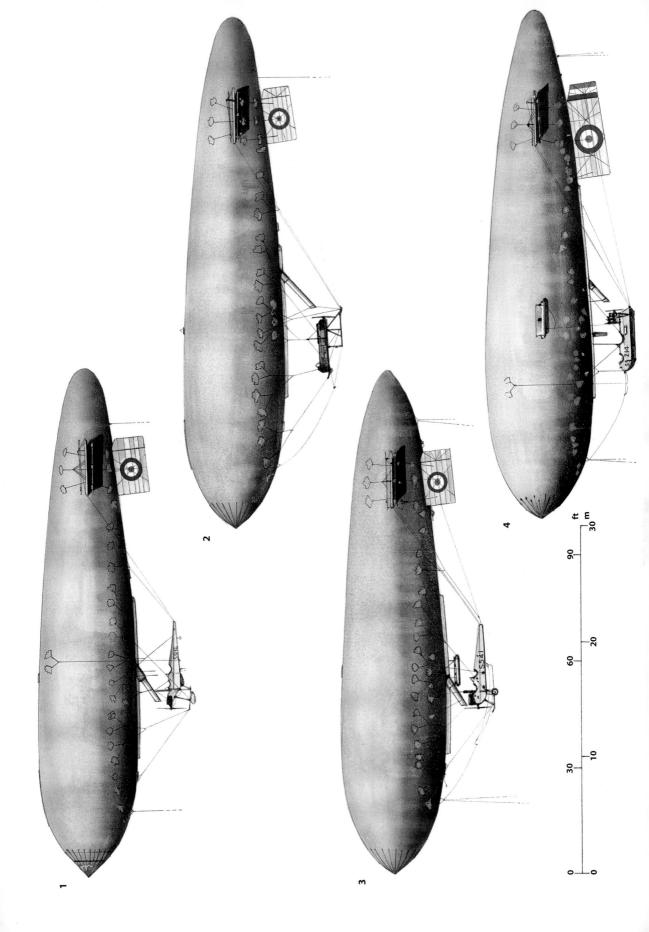

1

2

3

4

SS Z14

SS41

0   30   60   90   ft

0   10   20   30   m

Although the first Armstrong Whitworth SS type appeared in July 1915, the first of the production models did not follow until May 1916. The envelope capacity of the AW type was 70,000cu.ft, 10,000cu.ft more than the BE2c type, achieved by increasing the diameter of the envelope by 2ft 3in. – the length remaining the same. This photo shows an early version with four stabilizing planes.

Ltd and Armstrong Whitworth Ltd. Those present were invited to submit designs for a new non-rigid airship; it was to be designed for submarine detection work, be capable of an air speed of 40 to 50mph, with an endurance of up to eight hours while carrying a crew of two. It was to have a ceiling of 5000ft, carry wireless telegraphy (W/T) equipment and 160lb of bombs. The design was also required to be simple to facilitate rapid production, for the Admiralty wanted these new airships in the air within weeks. Three weeks later, a prototype built by the RNAS passed its flight trial, entering service as Submarine Scout 1 (SS.1).[1] The Airships Ltd prototype, designated SS.2, proved unsatisfactory and did not go into production.

Looking to what they had available, the RNAS team took the spare envelope of HMA No.2 and rigged it using *Eta* patches to the fuselage of a BE2c aircraft, having first removed the wings and tail unit. Although the lift produced was too low, the principle proved sound and production went ahead with an envelope of greater capacity.

The new rubberized fabric envelope received coatings of aluminium dope and varnish, giving a metallic look common to all subsequent British airships. It had a capacity of 60,000cu.ft, with an overall length of 143ft 5in. and a diameter of 27ft 9in. Inside were two ballonets, each with a capacity of 6,375cu.ft. There were four stabilizing planes fitted to the envelope, two fixed horizontally with elevators and two fitted radially below with rudders. Later models replaced the two lower planes with a single plane fitted centrally. The 24ft long BE2c fuselage was fitted with a 75hp Renault engine driving a four-bladed propeller, which produced a speed of 50mph. The pilot occupied the rear cockpit and the observer/W/T operator the front. The aircraft's

---

1 In some sources the term Sea Scout is used. However, in the official handbook published by the Admiralty in 1917 the name Submarine Scout is given.

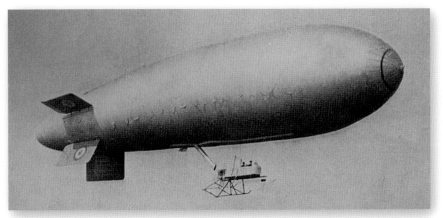

The Maurice Farman based SS type. Crews tended to prefer flying this version as they sat out of the propeller slipstream. In contrast to the other two SS types, the pilot occupied the front cockpit, with the observer/W/T operator behind, and, although dual controls were fitted, these were often removed to save weight. This shows an early version of the MF type with four stabilizing planes. later, most utilised three planes.

foot-operated rudder bar remained but a new vertical wheel was fitted in the cockpit to operate the elevators. Armament consisted of eight 16lb and two 65lb bombs.

In July 1915 an SS type airship produced by Armstrong Whitworth was commissioned as SS.27, using an Armstrong Whitworth FK.3 aircraft fuselage instead of the BE2c. With a greater capacity envelope (70,000cu.ft), the other main differences were a 100hp Green engine and petrol tanks that were slung from the envelope in fabric slings and suspended between the envelope and the car. This proved a more reliable method of delivering petrol to the engine than the integral tanks in the BE2c but increased drag, reducing top speed to 45mph. This type appears to have used three stabilizing planes.

Although their original design failed to get approval, Airships Ltd were contracted as one of the manufacturers of the new SS type airships and used Maurice Farman aircraft fuselages. These differed from the BE2c and Armstrong Whitworth in that they were a 'pusher' type, with the propeller positioned at the rear of the fuselage. Envelopes of either 60,000 or 70,000cu.ft were fitted, usually with three stabilizing planes. The engine, an 82hp Renault, drove a four-bladed propeller. Petrol was contained in a single 64gal tank positioned in front of the engine. Crews tended to prefer flying this type as they sat out of the propeller slipstream and were generally a little more comfortable, although top speed reached only 40mph. The pilot occupied the front cockpit with the observer/W/T operator behind.

Of the 49 SS type airships built during the war, 14 were sold overseas to the Italian and French governments.

Coastal (C) Class

Having rushed the SS class airships into service, the RNAS then turned its attention to developing an airship with increased endurance for extended patrols. The prototype was created using the envelope from HMA No.10, one of the Astra-Torres airships, employing its existing internal rigging to attach the large 170,000cu.ft trilobe envelope to a car created from the fuselages of two Avro 510 seaplanes. These were cut in half behind the cockpits and the two 'front' halves joined together, forming an extended four-seater car, 33ft 9in. long. Power was supplied by two 150hp Sunbeam engines, one positioned at each end, the forward engine working as a conventional 'tractor' and the rear one as a 'pusher'. Some later models replaced the rear engine with a 220hp Renault and the forward engine with a 100hp Berliet or Green. The first two Coastal airships entered naval service in January 1916.

The envelope was 195ft 6in. in length, with a diameter of 37ft. There were four internal ballonets, two in each of the lower envelope lobes, each with a capacity of 2,750cu.ft. At a top speed of 52mph the Coastal Class airships had an endurance of 11 hours, doubling to 22 hours when patrolling at half speed. The coxswain, who operated the rudder, occupied the forward cockpit, while the captain, who sat behind him, controlled the twin elevators. The W/T operator occupied the third seat while the engineer sat in the fourth. Between the captain and the W/T operator was a removable water ballast bag that could create space for an observer or passenger if required. Two petrol tanks, each carrying 110gal, were positioned in the car by the engines, but with the Renault engine fitted, the rear tank was moved to a position mounted on struts above the engineer. Later, C Class airships carried their fuel tanks in slings attached to the envelope. Armament consisted of either four 112lb or two 230lb bombs or depth charges, in addition to two Lewis guns, one fixed on the car and the other attached to a wooden frame laced to the top of the envelope, accessed via a tube running up through the envelope. Of the 32 C Class airships, the last completed in December 1916, five served overseas, four purchased by Russia and one by France.

B **THE QUEST FOR GREATER ENDURANCE**

The need for airships with a greater endurance, speed and climb than the rapidly produced SS type led to the development of a new non-rigid design. Again, existing equipment was utilised to create this new type, an Astra-Torres trilobe envelope of 170,000cu.ft being attached to a car created from the fuselages of two Avro 510 seaplanes. This resulted in the Coastal Class **(1)**, a most useful airship, although the arrangements for the crew were cramped and uncomfortable. Over 30 Coastals were built in 1916 but production then ended. Instead the RNAS began work on a new, improved airship, the North Sea Class **(2)**. The specification was for a further increase in endurance and reliability, greater lift and more comfort for the crew engaged in extended patrols. The envelope, again of trilobe design, was, at 360,000cu.ft, double the capacity of the Coastal, and the enclosed car allowed for the accommodation of two crews. However, the NS Class encountered a number of problems after the first five entered service in 1917, leading to a halt in production; it was May 1918 before it resumed. In the meantime an interim type filled the gap: the Coastal Star Class **(3)**. The C* had a larger, more streamlined trilobe envelope than the Coastal and improvements made to the car made life a little more comfortable for the crew. The first of ten C* airships entered service in February 1918 and all remained in service until October 1919.

Throughout this period work, commenced in 1914, continued on a rigid airship, HMA No.9r **(4)**, but it was only in April 1917 that it finally entered service. Although it had a gas capacity of 846,000cu.ft, its disposable lift and endurance only matched that of the much smaller North Sea Class non-rigid. No.9r had the honour of being the first flying British rigid but it was slow and unwieldy, being employed for the rest of the war as a training and experimental ship.

3

1

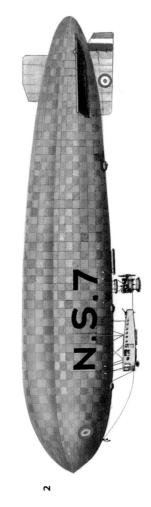

N.S.7

2

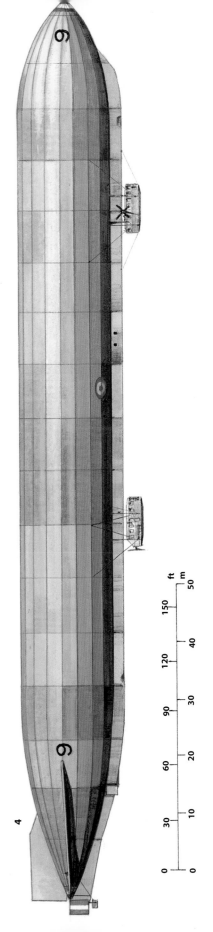

4

| ft | 0 | 30 | 60 | 90 | 120 | 150 |
| m | 0 | 10 | 20 | 30 | 40 | 50 |

Coastal Star (C*) Class

Work in 1917 to produce a new airship, the North Sea Class, with enhanced endurance encountered numerous problems and led to a halt in production after the first five entered service. In the meantime the RNAS developed an interim design at short notice. Known as the Coastal Star Class, a development of the C Class, the first appeared in early 1918.

A new envelope, which followed the trilobe form, increased in length to 207ft in the first three models, was extended further to 217ft in later models, with a width of 49ft 3in. Both types had a capacity of 210,000cu.ft. The introduction of six ballonets, three in each of the lower lobes, a large one positioned centrally and two smaller ones, one forward and one aft, led to improvements in control and stability. By fitting the engines, initially a 220hp Renault at the rear and 110hp Berliet forward, on extended mounts, the improved car offered more room for the crew. Later models used a 240hp Fiat rear engine. The canvas covering of the car was replaced with plywood, and four Triplex glass portholes were fitted on either side in addition to a glass floor panel, all intended to improve observation. The C* airships carried two Lewis guns, both fixed to the car. Other armament consisted of two 230lb and two 100lb bombs attached to frames on the car.

North Sea (NS) Class

Although the development of rigid airships had stalled, by 1915 it was underway again, but progress was slow. In the meantime work commenced on a class of non-rigids to tackle the problem of greatly extended patrols over the North Sea. This resulted in the North Sea Class. The first of this type, NS.1, appeared in February 1917 and was the largest of the non-rigid airships Britain produced. The envelope again followed the trilobe form but was 260ft long with a diameter of 57ft. This gave a capacity of 360,000cu.ft, double that of the C Class, and, as with the C* Class, six internal ballonets were fitted. There were four stabilizing planes, with elevators on the two horizontals and a rudder on the lower of the two vertical planes. Following the initial system of attaching the aluminium petrol tanks to the joints between the upper and lower lobes on the external surface of the envelope, a later development saw them relocated within the envelope. The fully enclosed car, constructed of light steel tubes covered with duralumin sheeting, contained a control room, navigation cabin and W/T cabin and had the

luxury of sleeping quarters for the crew of ten, divided into two five-man watches. To the rear of this main car, and connected to it by a canvas-covered wooden walkway, was the engineer's car. The original 250hp Rolls-Royce engines struggled with a complicated drive-shaft arrangement, but a change to two 240hp Fiat engines with direct drive to the propellers improved performance. In total 14 NS Class airships were completed, the last of these not entering service until March 1919. At a top speed of 57mph, the NS airships could remain in the air for 24 hours, but at lesser speeds patrols in excess of 48 hours were regularly undertaken.

Introduced in 1917 but not fully integrated until 1918, the North Sea airships generally carried three Lewis guns, two firing through windows in the control car and one fitted to a gun position on the top of the envelope. Four or six 230lb bombs were also carried. Although numbered NS.16, only 14 NS types were completed. NS.13 was renumbered as NS.14 and NS.15 was not delivered due to the Armistice.

Submarine Scout Pusher (SSP)

After the rushed introduction of the first SS airships, the RNAS began to look for ways to improve their design and performance. This resulted in the introduction of the SS Pusher Class in early 1917. Following the success of the Maurice Farman type, the newly designed car followed the same principle, with a rear-mounted 75hp Rolls-Royce Hawk engine giving a top speed of 52mph. Later, 100hp Green engines were fitted as the new Hawk engine had not yet achieved the reliability it later enjoyed. The car itself, about 25ft in length, was rectangular with a slightly rounded nose and a single landing skid. The SSP utilized the 70,000cu.ft capacity envelope used on the later SS models, with two aluminium petrol tanks slung from the sides. Only six SSP airships were built, entering service between January and June 1917.

Submarine Scout Zero (SSZ)

While RNAS Kingsnorth was developing the SSP as a successor to the SS Class, another team, at RNAS Capel, was involved in a similar project. Their design proved so successful that it led to the cancellation of the SSP Class. Like the SSP, the Zero also used the 70,000cu.ft envelope but the car was a completely new design, featuring many aspects of boat design, but still rigged to the envelope with Eta patches. By fitting an aluminium front cowl to the wooden frame of the car and covering the rest of the framework with plywood and a top layer of doped fabric, the whole car was rendered watertight. And with the bottom of the car designed like a ship's keel,

protected with copper sheeting, it enabled the Zeros to land on water and take off again. The three-man crew were positioned with the W/T operator (who also manned a Lewis gun) in the forward cockpit, the pilot in the centre and the engineer at the rear next to the engine. The engine, a 75hp Rolls-Royce Hawk, mounted on bearings above the surface of the car, drove a four-bladed pusher propeller. Having overcome initial problems, the Hawk was now a most efficient and reliable engine, the first British engine specifically designed for airships. With a top speed of 53mph, the SSZ Class also showed dramatic improvements in rate of climb and endurance over the SS Class. Fuel was held in two aluminium tanks suspended in the same manner as on the SSP Class. Besides the Lewis gun, Zeros also carried a number of bombs, initially two 65lb bombs, but later four 65lb or two 112lb bombs, one mounted on each side of the car, or one of 230lb were carried.

Submarine Scout Twin (SST)

Despite the successful introduction of the Zero, concerns remained over the vulnerability of single-engine airships to breakdown. Therefore experiments were carried out to develop a twin-engine model that could continue to function on one engine. Of three models, it was Submarine Scout Experimental (SSE) 2, developed at RNAS Mullion and also known as the 'Mullion Twin', that proved the more practical and became the prototype for the SS Twin Class.

The first of this last SS Class, SST.1, entered service in June 1918. It had a new envelope of 100,000cu.ft, with four ballonets and two air scoops, one working with each engine. Overall length of the new envelope was 165ft, with a diameter of 35ft 6in., and it was fitted with three stabilizing planes – an extended lower vertical one bearing the rudder, and two horizontal planes with elevators. With either 75hp Rolls-Royce Hawk or 100hp Sunbeam engines fitted, the SST Class delivered a top speed of 57mph. The now usual arrangement of two external fuel tanks slung on the envelope continued. The open, tapered, angular car had space for a crew of four or five. Although 115 SSTs were planned, the end of the war brought production to a halt with only 13 completed, numbered 1 to 14 (there was no 13 for reasons of superstition).

SEMI-RIGID (SR) AIRSHIPS

SR.1

The semi-rigid type of airship was never popular in Britain and the Navy purchased only one. This was an Italian-built M Class, which had a ceiling of 15,000ft and could carry up to half a ton bomb load – far more than any of the British non-rigids. A British crew arrived in Italy in July 1918 to carry out trials before flying it to Britain. Designated SR.1, it had an envelope with a capacity of 441,000cu.ft attached directly to a triangular-section tubular steel keel running the full length of the vessel. Overall length was 270ft, with a diameter of 55ft. Though it was normally fitted with two 220hp Italia engines, for the long flight to England an extra 200hp SPA-6a engine was fitted above the enclosed car. After a fraught three-day journey from Rome, SR.1 became the first aircraft of any type to complete this journey. It arrived at its assigned station, RNAS Pulham, on 6 November. Five days later the war ended. SR.1 was officially deleted from the airship fleet in September 1919.

The SSE.2 (or 'Mullion Twin'), one of three Submarine Scout Experimental airships. This model proved successful and became the prototype for the SST Class. Clearly shown in this photograph are the 'Eta patches' by which the car was attached to the envelope.

Having arrived in Britain in the final days of World War I, SR.1 – the Navy's only semi-rigid airship – saw its sole military service on 20 November 1918, forming part of the escort for the German U-boat fleet as it sailed in to surrender at Harwich.

RIGID AIRSHIPS

HMA No.9

The disastrous accident to HMA No.1, *Mayfly*, in September 1911 brought rigid airship development in Britain to an abrupt end. However, the apparent success of German rigids caused a rethink and the government gave the Admiralty approval to recommence a rigid airship programme in July 1915. Production had halted in early 1915 on HMA No.9r, originally ordered in 1913, but now resumed, although numerous delays continued to dog it throughout its construction. Only in November 1916 did it undertake its first test flight, and not until April 1917 was it accepted into service – already hopelessly outdated by rapid German airship advancement.

HMA No.9r reached a length of 526ft with a diameter of 53ft, its framework constructed of triangular-section duralumin girders. At the base of the frame a V-shaped keel ran the length of the ship, adding to the overall strength of the vessel. The centre of the keel opened out in a trapezium form where the W/T cabin and crew accommodation were located. Access to the keel from the two gondolas suspended below was by open ladder. Each enclosed gondola contained a control cabin and engine compartment, separated by a bulkhead. The engine compartments each housed two 180hp Wolseley-Maybach engines mounted on outriggers driving swivelling propellers. The seventeen gas-bags, made from rubberized cotton and lined with three layers of goldbeater's skin, held 846,000cu.ft of hydrogen. Two vertical and two horizontal stabilizing planes were fitted to the main framework, with the horizontals bearing triplane rudders and biplane elevators. Initially too heavy, it eventually gave a disposable lift of 3.8 tons, slightly in excess of that required in its original specification.

Later trials confirmed that at full speed of 45 mph No.9r gave an endurance of 18 hours, while at a cruising speed of 32 mph this extended to 50 hours. Armed with two Lewis guns, one attached to a car and the other on the top gun platform, and just three 100lb bombs, it performed at least one patrol over the North Sea and much experimental work, particularly relating to mooring systems. But its main value lay as a training ship for the crews that would fly in later rigid models. It was scrapped in June 1918.

23 Class

When, in July 1915, work recommenced on HMA No.9r, approval was also given for the development of an improved rigid airship known as the 23 Class. It was required to deliver a maximum speed of 55mph and disposable lift of 8 tons. The Admiralty approved Vickers' plans in October 1915 and

After initial trials HMA No.9r proved too heavy. To reduce weight, the two rear engines were removed and replaced with a single 250hp Maybach engine salvaged from the wreck of Zeppelin L.33. Other modifications involved reducing the gas-bag linings from three to two layers of goldbeater's skin. (Imperial War Museum Q.48008)

they immediately began work on the first of the class, No.23r. Plans were also distributed to Beardmore for No.24r and Armstrong Whitworth, who commenced work on No.25r; it was expected that a total of ten 23 Class airships would be built.

Although the 23 Class was largely based on No.9r, the major difference was the insertion of an additional transverse girder section to allow for an extra gas-bag. This added 9ft to the length while increasing gas capacity to 942,000cu.ft. The complex system of elevators and rudders used on No.9r gave way to the simpler expedient of attaching rudders and elevators directly to the two vertical and two horizontal stabilizing planes. The keel arrangement retained the central cabin but added a third gondola. The forward gondola contained a control cabin and engine room with a single 250hp Rolls-Royce Eagle powering a pair of swivelling 10ft-diameter propellers. A rear gondola was set up in exactly the same manner, with the control cabin reserved for emergency use, while the smaller midships gondola contained two Rolls-Royce Eagles, each driving a single fixed propeller.

In trials Nos. 23r, 24r and 25r all failed to deliver the required disposable lift. A fourth ship, R.26 (the Admiralty changed its numbering system for rigid airships in December 1917, the prefix R replacing the former suffix r), was then in production at Vickers and, in light of these problems, modifications were introduced and then applied to the first three as well. The main weight reduction was achieved by replacing the rear gondola with a smaller version with the engine driving only a single propeller. Despite all the changes, the 23 Class airships produced only 6.5 tons of disposable lift.

No.23r was the first British rigid to come under the public gaze when it flew over London in December 1917. *The Times* reported: 'There was something of majesty and beauty in its steady movement… [It] seemed to glide through the air with the smooth motion of a vast liner in an untroubled sea.' (Imperial War Museum Q.27575)

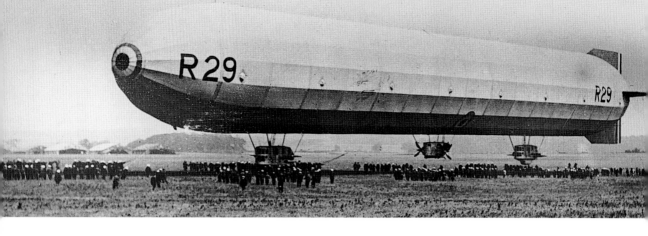

As to performance, at a maximum speed of 54mph the 23 Class could remain operational for 18 hours, while at the cruising speed of 38mph endurance extended to 50 hours.

The first three entered service in October 1917, joined by R.26 in April 1918, but further planned models were cancelled. Mainly used for training and experimental purposes, the 23 Class undertook only limited patrol work and all four were scrapped in 1919.

23X Class

In September 1916 Zeppelin L.33 came down in Essex with its framework virtually intact. Thus gaining access to the latest Zeppelin designs, the authorities realised that the 23 Class was outdated, so the last six of that class were cancelled and replaced with an order for four new airships of the 23X Class – numbered R.27 to R.30 – to incorporate some of these new ideas.

Gas capacity increased to 990,000cu.ft by minor changes to the framework that added 4ft to the length. Following tests, the most significant change was the removal of the external keel, which made great savings in weight and an improvement in manoeuvrability. The engine arrangement followed that used in the 23 Class design but incorporated a more recent

 THE DEVELOPMENT OF THE RIGIDS

Although Britain had been slow to enter the field of rigid airship design, the perceived success of German rigids ensured that development gained momentum in 1915. Building on the lessons learnt during the construction of No.9r, work was authorised on a new type, the 23 Class **(1)**, in October of that year. Essentially a lengthened version of 9r, the 23 Class, with a capacity of 942,000cu.ft, offered almost 100,000cu.ft more than 9r. But delays meant that it was not until two years later, in October 1917, that the first three ships of this four-ship class entered service. None of the four attained a level of performance significantly in excess of that of 9r and all were employed mainly in a training and experimental role.

Initially all British rigid airship construction had followed designs put forward by Vickers, but the 31 Class (R.31 and R.32) **(2)**, designed by Short Brothers, differed from its predecessors by using a wooden framework. With a capacity of 1,500,000cu.ft, good speed and a high disposable lift, the 31 Class showed great promise although there were concerns regarding the strength of its wooden girders. But R.31, the first of the class, did not enter service until five days before the end of the war, so the potential was never fully tested.

The final British rigid airship, the massive R.101 **(3)**, was one of two built to operate a cross-Empire airship service. Its total capacity was 5,500,000cu.ft, and a hundred airships the size of Britain's first, *Nulli Secundus*, could have been fitted inside the envelope of R.101. Built by the government's Air Ministry, the R.101 incorporated many new and innovative features but, owing to a strict timetable, testing was restricted before it departed on its ill-fated first flight to British India in October 1930. Its loss spelt the end of airship development in Britain.

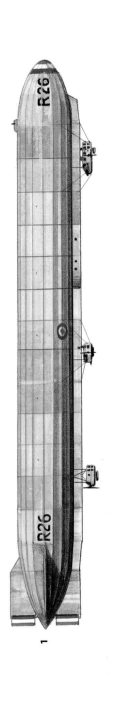

R26

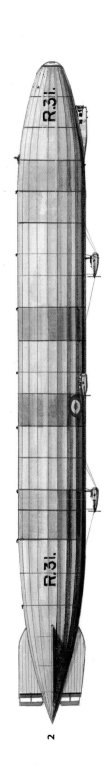

R.31.

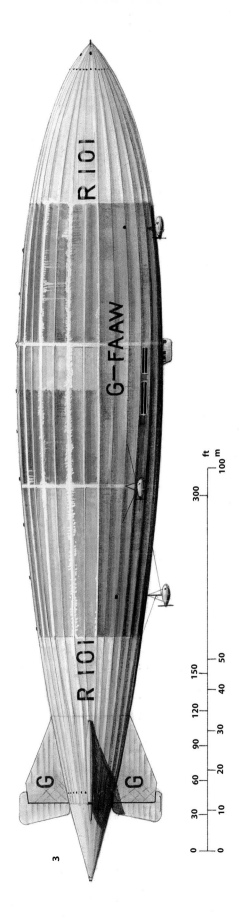

R 101

G—FAAW

ft	m
	100
300	
	50
150	40
120	30
90	20
60	
30	10
0	0

1

2

3

Rolls-Royce Eagle model, each engine producing 300hp. The first two ships, R.27 (built by Beardmore) and R.29 (Armstrong Whitworth), received commissions in June 1918, having impressed with a disposable lift of 8.5 tons during trials. However, further investigation of the wreckage of L.33 led to the cancellation of R.28 and R.30 as plans developed to build a new class based on this latest information.

Fire destroyed R.27 as it lay in its shed at Howden in August 1918 after just two months' service. However, R.29 had far more success and took part in three separate U-boat attacks in the North Sea. Having flown over 11,000 miles in service, R.29 was finally deleted from the service in October 1919.

R.31 Class

Until the decision by the Admiralty to give the go-ahead for the design of the R.31 Class, all British rigid airships had come from the designs of Vickers. Now, Short Brothers built the first of this class, R.31, at their new facility at Cardington, Bedfordshire, the design being based on those of the German firm Schütte-Lanz, which specialised in wooden-framed airships.

Overall R.31 extended to a length of 615ft with a diameter of 65ft 6in. Its envelope held 21 gas-bags with a total capacity of 1,500,000cu.ft, a 50 per cent increase over the 23X Class, achieving 16.5 tons disposable lift. The framework, constructed of wooden three-ply triangular-section girders, with its tapering tail section gave a more streamlined shape overall than previous designs. The control car demonstrated an innovative design in that it extended forward from the lower girders, giving direct access to the internal walkway, this being possible as all six 300hp Rolls-Royce Eagle engines were contained in separate streamlined cars arranged in pairs along the ship.

At its first trial in the summer of 1918 R.31 surprised everyone with a top speed of 70mph. With this in mind, and the high fuel consumption recorded, the removal of one of the rear engines resulted in a speed reduction of only 5mph but at the same time increased disposable lift to 19 tons. Not commissioned into service until 6 November 1918, just five days before the end of the war, R.31 experienced stress problems in some of its wooden girders on the way to its station at East Fortune, Scotland. Forced to land at Howden in Yorkshire, it suffered further damage while housed there, putting it beyond repair. This then led in turn to dismantling work commencing in February 1919.

R.31 had a short active life. Framework stress problems discovered on its delivery flight forced it to land at Howden, where it was housed in a shed damaged by fire three months earlier. There, rain leaking through the roof repairs caused critical damage to the wooden framework. (Imperial War Museum Q. 48023)

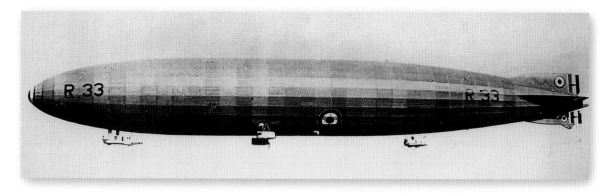

Much delayed by the changing circumstances at the end of the war, R.32, the second and last of the R.31 Class, finally received its commission in September 1919. When the Royal Air Force took over responsibility for airships from the Navy the following month, it handed R.32 over to the National Physical Laboratory (NPL) for experimental work, before, in March 1920, it headed to Howden for use as a training ship. By April 1921, no longer required, R.32 was dismantled, and its framework was tested to destruction by the NPL.

As part of its commercial programme R.33 took part in a series of mooring mast tests in extreme conditions. These tests proved the viability of the mast and removed the need for large expensive sheds at each landing field.

R.33 Class

The steady flow of information gleaned from the wreckage of Zeppelin L.33 curtailed the 23X Class and led to the R.33 Class, two airships that were close copies of the German vessel. However, it took many months for the technicians and designers to unravel and then reconstruct L.33's secrets, with neither airship ready to take to the sky until March 1919. Armstrong Whitworth built R.33 while Beardmore constructed R.34. They were identical in design and saw a return to metal construction. Each ship reached a length of 643ft with a diameter of 76ft. The envelope contained 19 gas-bags, giving a capacity of 1,950,000cu.ft and disposable lift of 26 tons. Each had five 240hp Sunbeam Maori 4 engines, giving a maximum speed of 62mph. One engine was contained in a separate compartment directly behind the control car, two were in cars positioned midships – one either side of the centre axis, and an aft engine car contained two engines geared to a single propeller.

Once accepted into service, R.33 moved to Pulham, where it was detailed for scouting duty over the North Sea. In fact, R.33 undertook a number of long-range flights over the United Kingdom, as well as promotional flights in Britain and Europe. In 1920 responsibility for airships passed to the Air Council, which began a programme of testing aimed at commercial development. Thus R.33 received the civilian registration G-FAAB.

In 1921, in the wake of the shocking R.38 disaster, the government ordered a halt to all further airship development and R.33 avoided the scrapheap only because of its civilian status. It remained in its shed at Cardington until the launch of a new airship research policy in 1924. Refitted and reconditioned, R.33 provided important research data for the new massive rigid airships, the R.100 and R.101. It continued to give valuable service until November 1926, when, with its framework beginning to show signs of fatigue, it was laid up before dismantling work commenced in 1928.

Its sister ship, the R.34, entered service in May 1919. For details of its record-breaking career see colour plate D, page 32.

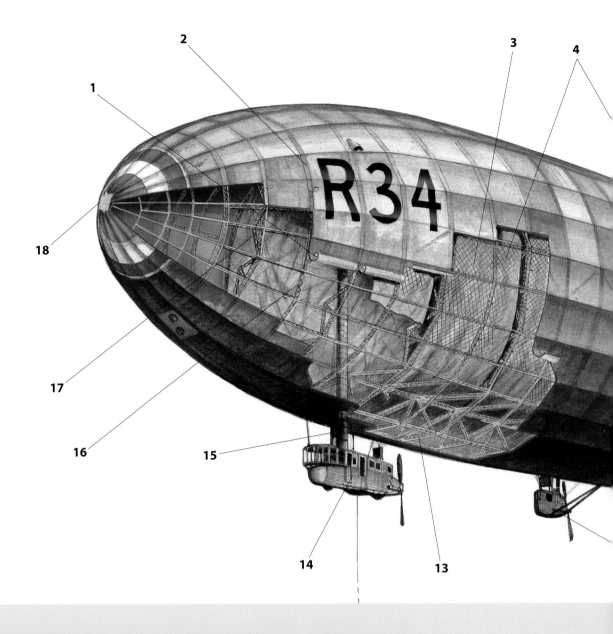

D R.34: THE FIRST TRANSATLANTIC ROUND TRIP

The R.34, the sister ship to R.33, entered service in May 1919 after encountering a number of problems during its flight trials. Following an endurance flight of 54 hours in June 1919, authorisation was given to commence final preparations for a flight to America. In the early hours of 2 July 1919, R.34 left East Fortune, Scotland, and headed west, destination New York. Encountering strong headwinds, the crew began to fear that their fuel would not hold out for the journey but they carefully nursed the engines and R.34 safely arrived on Long Island after a flight of 108 hours. It was the first east–west aerial crossing of the Atlantic, achieved just three weeks after Alcock and Brown's aeroplane crossing on the west–east route. Three days later R.34 headed homewards, covering the return distance aided by strong tail winds in 75 hours, and, redirected to Pulham, completed the first aerial round trip from Britain to America and back.

After a six-month refit R.34 moved between East Fortune, Pulham and Howden, from where it set off on a training flight on 21 January 1921. Caught in bad weather, R.34 struck a hill on the North Yorkshire Moors and damaged two propellers. It limped home to Howden on half power but strong winds prevented it entering its shed. Having abandoned ship, the crew moored it in the open but further strong gusts of wind during the night battered it to the ground. In the morning R.34 lay damaged beyond repair. Within a few days the buckled framework of this great aerial pioneer was hacked into pieces and sold for scrap.

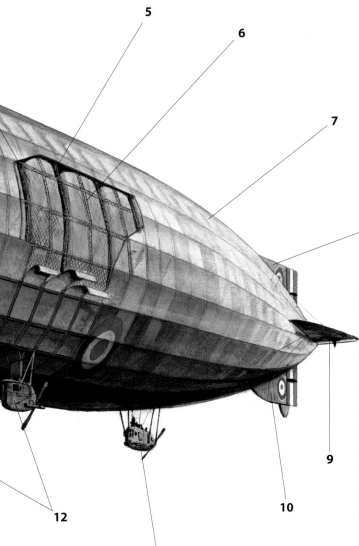

5

6

7

8

9

10

12

11

TECHNICAL DATA

Type R.34

Overall Length 643ft

Max. Diameter 79ft

Overall Height 92ft

Engines 5 x 250hp Sunbeam Maori 4

Est. Max. Speed 62mph

Cruising Speed 45mph

Max Speed Achieved 55mph

Gas Capacity 1,950,000cu.ft

Gross Lift 59 tons

Disposable Lift 26 tons

KEY

1 Strips of linen fabric laced to frame girders to form envelope.

2 Narrow linen fabric strips glued to seal envelope strips.

3 Cord mesh to prevent gasbags chafing against girders.

4 Gasbags (19 in total).

5 Main circumferential frame girder.

6 Auxiliary circumferential frame girder.

7 Envelope aluminium doped to reflect sunlight and reduce gas expansion.

8 Tail fin with rudder.

9 Tail plane with elevator.

10 Tail fin with rudder.

11 Rear power car containing two engines driving single propeller.

12 Wing power cars, each containing one engine.

13 Keel; running length of airship containing narrow walkway, living space and storage.

14 Control car or gondola. Front section contains control room and wireless cabin, rear section contains a single engine.

15 Access tube to observation platform/gun platform.

16 Auxiliary circumferential frame girder.

17 Main circumferential frame girder.

18 Nose crest: Arms of Scotland.

On 2 July 1919 R.34 left East Fortune heading for Long Island, New York, completing the crossing of the Atlantic in 108 hours. Three days later R.34 headed homewards, covering the return journey, aided by strong tail winds, in 75 hours, to complete the first aerial round trip across the Atlantic.

R.36

With work underway on R.33 and R.34, the government approved a budget for three more airships (R.35, R.36 and R.37) in January 1917, but only R.36 survived later cuts. Six months after approval of the project, an investigation of Zeppelin L.48, brought down over Suffolk, discovered it to be of the very latest design, and development of the new airships ceased while a detailed analysis of the wreckage took place. As a result, R.36 was lengthened to accommodate an additional gas cell to give it a targeted ceiling of 17,000ft.

During the lengthy development process, R.36 also incorporated design knowledge gleaned from Zeppelin L.49, which came down in France in October 1917, as well as technical information obtained from the Zeppelin works after the war. When R.36 finally took to the air in April 1921 it reached a length of 675ft with a diameter just under 79ft. The envelope held 2,101,000cu.ft of hydrogen and delivered a disposable lift of 16 tons. Five engines supplied the power: three 350hp Sunbeam Cossacks and two 260hp Maybach engines recycled from Zeppelin L.71, handed over to Britain as part of war reparations. Although conceived as a military airship, by the time it

With the decision to complete R.36 as a civil aircraft, extensive modifications were required which included fitting a passenger car containing 25 double berths, a galley, lavatories and a storage area for provisions and luggage. (Imperial War Museum Q.48030)

The R.38, built at the Royal Airship Works, Cardington, for the United States Navy, had a length of 699ft and a diameter of 86ft. The gas capacity reached 2,724,000cu.ft. Six 350hp Sunbeam Cossack engines supplied the power, attaining a speed of 71mph.

reached completion three years after the end of the war, it carried the civilian registration G-FAAF. Damaged in June 1921 at Pulham, R.36 entered its shed for repairs but there it remained, affected, like R.33, by the R.38 disaster. Eventually, in June 1926, the order came for it to be scrapped.

R.38

In June 1918 the Admiralty issued requirements for a series of long-range high-altitude airships with a ceiling of 22,000ft. The order for the first of these, R.38, was given to Short Brothers at Cardington, while orders for three sister ships, R.39, R.40 and R.41, were placed with Armstrong Whitworth and Beardmore. Work began on R.38 in February 1919 but the post-war economy caused the cancellation of its sister ships. Indeed, following the nationalisation of Cardington in April 1919 as the Royal Airship Works (RAW), R.38 became the subject of cancellation discussions until interest by the United States Navy in purchasing a long-range airship changed the situation. In October 1919 revised plans were produced and, although these were for a new ship, some parts of R.38 and the cancelled R.40 were incorporated in the design. Then, in a change from normal numbering policy, it retained the original R.38 designation. Its first three trial flights in June and July 1921 revealed a number of faults that were rectified, but pressure to hand R.38 over to its American crew mounted and determined that its fourth would be its final test flight. Bearing its new United States Navy designation, ZRII, it set off from Howden with a crew of 49 on board, including 17 Americans, to carry out tests over the North Sea. Bad weather prevented it from landing at Pulham as intended and while on its way back to Howden on 24 August 1921, as it undertook a series of vigorous course alterations over the mouth of the River Humber, R.38 crumpled in the middle and two explosions ripped it apart. There were only five survivors. The destruction of the R.38 brought an abrupt end to Britain's involvement in military airship production.

R.80

The last rigid airship ordered during World War I was the R.80, designated outside the standard numbering system. Work began in November 1917 on what is considered the most streamlined of all British rigid airships. Although the demand now was for bigger airships, the R.80 attained a length of only

No sooner had R.80 been delivered to Howden than it was considered for scrapping as a result of the post-war economic downturn. However, it received a stay of execution when allocated to the American crew training for the R.38.

535ft, its size restricted by the limited capacity of Vickers' Walney Island facilities. With a diameter of 70ft, the envelope had a gas capacity of 1,200,000cu.ft. Four 230hp Wolseley-Maybach engines provided the power, two positioned behind the streamlined control car driving a single propeller, and the other two in single engine cars positioned midships. Disposable lift reached approximately 16 tons. In 1919 the government decided the unfinished R.80 no longer had any military value, but production continued as there were hopes for a commercial future. Its first flight took place in the summer of 1920 and nearly ended in disaster when the ship rose too fast, causing buckling of a number of the framework girders. Its second flight did not take place until January 1921 and in February it was flown to its base at Howden. Its last flight took place in September 1921 when it flew to Pulham, being used there in scientific tests until destroyed.

R.100 and R.101

In 1924 the government announced a new research programme, giving birth to the Imperial Airship Scheme, a plan to link the British Empire by long-range airship routes. The scheme authorised the building of two massive airships, each with a capacity of 5,000,000cu.ft, a disposable lift of 50 tons and accommodation for 100 passengers. The previous numbering system having been abandoned, one ship, built by the civilian Airship Guarantee Company based at Howden, with Barnes Wallis as chief designer, was designated the R.100. Later to earn renown as the inventor of the World War II 'bouncing bomb', Barnes Wallis had also worked as a designer on No.9r and R.80. The government-owned Royal Airship Works at Cardington built the second, the R.101, the design team being headed by LtCol Vincent Richmond.

The R.100 (civil registration G-FAAV) made its first flight in December 1929 from Howden to Cardington, from where it undertook a number of test flights over the next six months. It had a capacity of 5,156,000cu.ft with a length of 709ft and a 130ft diameter, with power supplied by six 660hp Rolls-Royce Condor IIIB engines contained in three engine cars, two positioned midships and one to the rear. The three floors of passenger accommodation were suspended inside the envelope. On 29 July 1930 the R.100 departed on a successful transatlantic flight to Canada, but on its return, while it was laid up for repairs, dramatic events elsewhere ensured that it never flew again.

The R.101 (civil registration G-FAAW) featured many innovative designs, including a framework of stainless steel instead of duralumin, and carried the two levels of passenger accommodation as an integral part of the overall framework. The initial design was 735ft long with a diameter of 131ft, giving it a capacity of 4,893,740cu.ft, but, after its first flight, it produced only about 35 tons of disposable lift, 15 tons short of target. Part of this weight problem was caused by the use of heavy – believed safer – diesel engines instead of the usual petrol-driven types. There were five of these 600hp Beardmore Tornado engines, each in an individual car. Steps taken to lighten the ship increased lift by 9 tons but some of these changes exacerbated other problems that were becoming apparent. However, there was significant pressure to ensure that R.101, as the government airship, was ready for its maiden Empire-crossing flight, scheduled for September 1930, on which the Air Minister, Lord Thompson, intended to fly. To increase lift further, a late decision added a new section of framework, allowing the insertion of an additional gas-bag. This change increased the length by 42 feet and gave a new gas capacity of 5,509,753cu.ft, which finally delivered the required lift. R.101 undertook eleven trial flights, which unearthed additional problems that needed time to rectify fully. However, because of time restraints, many of these received only rudimentary repairs.

In the end R.101, issued with a temporary certificate of airworthiness, departed for Karachi, then in British India (now Pakistan), on 4 October 1930. On board was a crew of 42, plus six officials from the RAW and six other passengers, including Lord Thompson. Almost as soon as it took to the air it encountered problems, both technically and with the weather. It struggled on over northern France until the early hours of the following morning, when, already flying at very low altitude, it began to dive. The nose was brought up and the ship levelled but then began a shallow dive, forcing it down, quite gently, into a hillside near Beauvais, about 40 miles north of Paris. Moments later, blinding, searing flames engulfed the wreckage as

The R.100, one of two airships built as part of the Imperial Airship Scheme. It departed on its inaugural flight to Montreal, Canada, on 29 July 1930, completing the journey in a little under 79 hours. The return flight, with the benefit of prevailing winds, took just 58 hours. (Imperial War Museum H[AM]531)

The doomed R.101 leaving the Cardington mooring mast during its troubled trials. Passengers boarded the airship by taking a lift to the top of the mast and entering via a gangway let down under the nose.

5,500,000cu.ft of hydrogen gas exploded. Of the 54 people on board, only six, all members of the crew, escaped the blazing inferno with their lives.

In Britain there was great national mourning and a state funeral for those who died in the wreckage. The crash marked the end for Britain's airship development. The government withdrew any further backing for a rigid airship programme and thus closed the door on a quarter of a century of aerial experimentation, ingenuity and innovation.

BRITISH AIRSHIPS AT WAR

The threat posed to Britain's trade routes by Germany's submarines in World War I was the catalyst that, from February 1915, accelerated the development and deployment of British airships.

The main task for these airships was, by using their height and speed advantage, to locate the presence of an enemy submarine and call for support from surface vessels. In addition, airships carried a limited armament of bombs with which to engage enemy submarines and machine guns for use against enemy mines. The airship crews, however, spent the majority of their time on seemingly endless patrols, scanning the vastness of an empty ocean for signs of the enemy. Not only the obvious sight of a submarine on the surface, but the trail of a periscope or even small amounts of oil on the sea could give away a submarine's presence – as could the behaviour of seagulls. Vigilance was the key – for hours on end, exposed to all the conditions that Britain's weather can offer.

The typical tactics employed on convoy patrol are demonstrated in a report given by Capt T. P. Moore, while commanding C.9 from Mullion, south Cornwall. On 26 March 1918, having been on patrol off the Isles of Scilly for over six hours, Moore received a radio message directing him to escort in an American convoy. In his report Moore states:

> C.9 proceeded to keep about half to three quarters of a mile from the convoy on the sunny side, at times crossing the head of the convoy in order to search

for possible drifting mines etc., but mainly passing up and down the sunny (starboard) side as being the most likely field of attack. Occasionally dropped astern a little in case of a submarine having passed under the length of the convoy for a stern attack.

While most patrols made no enemy sightings, when they did they produced sudden bursts of intense excitement. Another Coastal Class airship from Mullion, C.22, had an encounter with a submarine on 12 February 1917. Alerted by a steamer that another ship had been torpedoed earlier, C.22, commanded by FltSubLt C. S. Coltson, began to sweep the area. After almost two hours scanning the surface, Coltson spotted a submarine surfacing about one mile off his port side. He reported that:

Endless airship patrols were spent in search of tell-tale signs such as this – the periscope wake and oil trail of a U-boat.

When her conning tower was above the surface, and the wash of the hull just becoming visible, she must have sighted the Airship, and made all haste to submerge again. I had meanwhile altered course towards her and opened out to full speed. She had just succeeded in submerging when I got over the spot and the first bomb I dropped fell some way ahead of her and failed to explode. By putting my helm hard over I was able to release my second bomb almost immediately after; this was as near a direct hit as possible, the explosion with delay action fuse, directly over the swirl left by the conning tower of the submarine. A large quantity of oil came to the surface as well as numerous small bubbles. Nothing further was seen of the submarine. The bombs were dropped from a height of 1000 feet... I remained in the immediate vicinity for close on two hours, and later for another two hours swept an area with a radius of about 15 miles from the spot. There were, however, no signs of the submarine, which I believe to have been sunk by the second bomb.

It was surprisingly difficult to discern if a submarine had been hit during an attack. An account by FltLt R. S. Montague of a patrol in C.23A on 17 November 1917 illustrates the difficulty, despite textbook co-operation between air and surface vessels. Having spotted two ships and an extensive area of wreckage, C.23A investigated, receiving information of the torpedoing of another ship. Cruising around, Montague believed he spotted a submerged submarine making 3–4 knots about a mile from the wreckage. From a height of 800ft he dropped two 100lb bombs, after which air bubbles began to rise. One of the surface vessels, an armed trawler, came up and dropped a depth charge over the bubbles. Directed by flares dropped by C.23A, the trawler launched a further six depth charges, which increased the flow of bubbles and oil reaching the surface but produced no wreckage. Having run out of flares, Montague continued to indicate the position by firing a Lewis gun at the sea. The trawler dropped two more depth charges, bringing more oil to the surface, and then a motor launch joined them, launching two depth charges, which brought forth another rush of bubbles and a little more oil. However, with no clear confirmation of the presence of any enemy submarine, C.23A returned to base after a patrol of 9 hours 45 minutes.

The weather also conspired against the airships in their war against the U-boats. On 23 January 1918, C.19 was on patrol in dense fog over the North

A Coastal Class airship (C.23A) patrolling above a convoy searching for enemy submarines and mines. The convoy system was introduced in the summer of 1917.

Sea when it received a signal giving the position of a submarine on the surface. C.19 proceeded to the area and, finding a break in the fog, held a position on the edge of the fog bank for about 30 minutes, when a submarine appeared below. Her commander reported:

> A submarine with conning tower awash was observed at a distance of one and a half miles... Course was set at full speed for the submarine, which immediately started to submerge, disappearing 30 seconds before the airship was over her. The swirl was distinctly visible, and the submarine altered course to port on submerging. Two 100lb bombs were dropped, the first 60 yards short due to the bomb dropping on turning the dropping toggle preparatory to pulling. The second one dropped about 20 yards ahead and to port of the swirl. A quantity of air came up 10 yards ahead of position where the bomb exploded. The airship remained in the vicinity for half an hour, but owing to the fog closing in immediately nothing more could be seen.

E   **AIRSHIP VERSUS U-BOAT**

On the morning of 7 December 1917, SSZ.16 left the airship base at Pembroke on a routine patrol over the Irish Sea. Captained by FltLt John E. Barrs, she was heading home at 15.55 when a submarine came into view on the surface about a mile away. Barrs turned his Zero towards the submarine in an attempt to identify it, climbing to gain height in case the submarine was hostile. Closely watching for a recognition signal, Barrs then saw the submarine turn towards his airship. Moments later the deck gun of the U-boat opened fire. Barrs immediately ordered the W/T operator, F. E. Tattersall, to return fire with the Lewis gun. So effectively did he sweep the deck that the U-boat immediately prepared to dive, leaving the crew no time to fire a second round before dashing for safety. Arriving over the submarine's position about a minute after it submerged, SSZ.16 dropped two 65lb bombs, each with a 2.5-second delay fuse. The first bomb landed about 25ft off the port bow of the U-boat and exploded on or near the surface; the second fell closer but failed to explode. The engineer, J. W. Trevelyn, then dropped calcium flares over the side to mark the spot as Barrs took the decision to turn for home as darkness and a blanketing sea mist began to gather. Passing two destroyers making for the flares, Barrs paused to brief them before continuing on to Milford Haven, where, with his W/T transmitter out of service, he sent details of the engagement ashore by Aldis lamp before he finally returned to Pembroke. Barrs later received the Distinguished Service Cross for his actions.

Those who crewed the SSZ Class airships much appreciated their manoeuvrability and this is clearly demonstrated in this example, which again highlights the liaison between airships and surface craft. Taking off from Folkestone on 3 January 1918, SSZ.5, commanded by FltSubLt W. J. Pullen, received a signal from a patrol boat that it had dropped a depth charge in the vicinity of an enemy submarine and the captain asked if the airship could observe any result. SSZ.5 flew over the area, observing traces of oil, then three large air bubbles followed by a larger circular patch of oil. Pullen concluded that the depth charge had been effective. Then, another patrol boat approached and Pullen informed them that he believed he was over a submerged, damaged submarine. While the captain of the newly arrived patrol boat prepared to drop depth charges, Pullen described his actions:

> I then descended within eight feet of the water, and showed the exact position by steering along the course made by the oil and making a right angle turn when directly over the place at which the oil was rising. Three depth charges were then dropped… I consider that the third charge was effective as much larger quantities of oil were observed to rise to the surface and continued to do so for some time.

However, the airship crews did not have it all their own way. On a few occasions the hunted became the hunter. On 17 March 1918 FltLt R. S. Montague was again in command of C.23A. While patrolling over the English Channel, at 13.20 Montague observed a submarine about 3 miles away. Almost immediately the submarine opened fire from its deck gun, the first shot bursting half a mile short and the second about 400 yards short. Having taken stock of the situation, Montague then reported:

> I decided it was impossible to attack the submarine up wind at 350 feet. C.23a rose to 900 feet, two shrapnel bursts being heard below as the ship entered the clouds. I proceeded up wind in clouds. Owing to the difficulty of steering in clouds and the impossibility of getting above them … C.23a proceeded full out for ten minutes up wind. At 13.30 I decided the ship was as near as possible over the submarine. C.23a descended at maximum speed and when at 700 feet the surface of the sea was observed in a break in the clouds, no sign of the submarine was observed until a shrapnel burst between 40 and 50 yards astern of the ship. It could not be observed in which direction the submarine lay and I concluded that a further descent would be impossible for attack as the submarine had already sighted C.23a.

The wreckage of SSZ.27 towed in by armed trawler *Kinaldie* after becoming a victim of 'friendly fire' from the trawler *Marne II*.

Montague immediately climbed back up to 1600ft and tried to manoeuvre for a better chance of attack but noticed the envelope was losing pressure. Believing at first that shrapnel had holed the envelope, he abandoned the attack and set course for land, only discovering later that a faulty valve had caused the loss of gas.

The crew of C.23A survived their encounter; another crew to have a lucky escape was that of SSZ.27. While patrolling over the English Channel off the southern Cornish coast on 12 April 1918, SSZ.27 spotted a floating mine and opened up with a Lewis gun to try to destroy it. Attracted by the firing, C.9 approached and opened fire too, but still the mine did not explode. Two armed trawlers then arrived and, believing the airships were indicating the presence of a submarine with their gunfire, one of them, the *Marne II*, dropped two depth charges, oblivious to the mine now floating just a couple of yards off its port bow. Captain Arthur Elliot brought SSZ.27 down close to the trawler and advised her captain of the danger. The trawler turned away hard one way and SSZ.27 the other. Much to Elliot's surprise, the trawler then 'opened fire at mine with Forward Gun when I was right across her bows about 100 yards away from him and height 200ft'. Moments later the airship lost gas pressure and began 'falling like a stone' into the sea. The second trawler picked up the crew and an inquiry later confirmed they were victims of 'friendly fire', caused by a ricochet or splinter from the single shell fired at the mine by the *Marne II*.

FltLt E. F. Monk, who survived an extraordinary and perilous journey across the Bristol Channel clinging to the axle of SS.42.

FltLt Errol F. Monk had a most extraordinary escape while commanding SS.42 on a routine patrol from Pembroke on 15 September 1916. The patrol started normally but, with an increasing squally wind, Monk decided to return to base. As he touched down, a strong gust caught SS.42 side on, lifting it 30ft into the air before smashing it down on its port side, breaking most of the suspension cables on that side and almost completely overturning the car. Monk and his wireless operator clung on desperately but then SS.42 began to rise rapidly, helped, as Monk recalled unsympathetically, 'by the wireless operator falling out when about 20 feet above the ground'. The ship continued to climb and had reached 1000ft by the time Monk had clambered on top of the upturned car, where, unable to control it, he had 'no alternative but to sit where I was … and trust to luck'. SS.42 drifted out over the Bristol Channel, climbing all the time. As he approached Lundy Island, Monk estimated his altitude at 7,000ft. And then things got even worse:

> About this time the forward suspensions on the starboard side which were supporting most of the weight of the engine broke and the car fell into a vertical position, engine down, nearly pitching me from my precarious hold, but with great difficulty I clambered down and found a seat on the axle of the undercarriage.

SS.42 continued climbing until Monk estimated he was at 8,400ft, at which point he started to drop slowly at first but then with increasing speed until he calculated he was falling at between 1,000 and 1,500ft per minute. His nightmarish journey finally ended when he crashed near the village of Ermington in Devon, about 100 miles from Pembroke. Monk was badly injured, fracturing his spine, but ten months later, fully recovered from his hair-raising journey, he returned to duty.

While some crews, such as those of SSZ.27 and SS.42, had lucky escapes, inevitably other crews paid the ultimate price. On 11 December 1917 C.27

left its base at Pulham to patrol over the North Sea but failed to return; its last radio transmission was timed at 09.25 – then silence. The following day a trawler captain reported having seen an airship on fire at about 09.30. By the time he reached the scene there was no trace of the airship other than a small piece of wreckage floating on the surface. Later information revealed that a German Hansa-Brandenburg W12 seaplane, one of a flight of three, had pounced on C.27 and shot it down in flames. The pilot, FltLt J. F. Dixon, DSC, and his four-man crew were all lost.

SUMMARY

At the outbreak of World War I Britain possessed seven airships, all largely experimental. During the period of the war another 218 were produced, of which 103 were still flying at the time of the Armistice. Britain's airship fleet recorded about 89,000 flying hours and covered over 2 million miles around Britain's coastal waters, escorting convoys, patrolling and acting as a deterrent to Germany's hostile submarine fleet. Records indicate that during the war U-boats sank only one ship that was being escorted by an airship.

Only in 1915 did the government first acknowledge the need for a fleet of airships as a weapon against the raiding U-boats, but it required them to be produced cheaply and built quickly. By the end of the war Britain was investing vast sums in the production of large rigid airships but these contributed very little to the war effort in comparison to the non-rigid designs. In the last 17 months of the war (June 1917 to October 1918) airships sighted 49 enemy submarines and were involved in attacks on 27. In addition they located 134 mines, of which 73 were destroyed. The airship service lost 48 men in the line of duty during the war.

Germany had attempted to defeat Britain by cutting its maritime supply lines by the aggressive use of its submarine fleet, but the tireless work of the airship service, in conjunction with the ships of the Royal Navy prevented them from achieving their goal.

PROBLEMS ON PATROL

While on patrol over the Bristol Channel on the morning of 18 January 1917 the engine of SS.15 started giving problems. Then the captain, SubLt Cyril J. Pyke, reported that it 'gave two coughs' and the revs fell alarmingly; it then gave one more cough and stopped. While Pyke fired Very lights to attract the attention of naval vessels based at nearby Tenby, he ordered his W/T operator, Frederick Crawford, to climb out on to the narrow landing skid to try to start the engine by swinging the propeller. This was only Crawford's second flight and later he admitted that he had never started an engine before. He was now attempting this task for the first time 1,500ft up in the air in a 15-knot wind balanced on a narrow strip of wood just 2½ inches wide. Unsurprisingly Crawford failed. Pyke ordered him back in and he himself then clambered out from the rear seat and down on to the skid, spending the next 45 minutes attempting to start the engine, but without success. Having returned to the cockpit and climbed to 2,700ft as they drifted towards Lundy Island, Pyke then climbed out again, attempting once more to coax the engine back into life. Unnoticed initially by either Pyke or Crawford, SS.15 began to fall, slowly at first, then with increasing speed. As soon as he did notice, Pyke clambered back into his seat but was unable to halt its fall and it 'struck the water hard'. As the envelope began to settle down on top of them, Pyke ordered Crawford overboard while he unsuccessfully attempted to deflate it, before joining him in the water. As he cleared the wreckage, Pyke noticed Crawford was still clinging to the car, his feet tangled in the control lines. Fortunately, a motor launch arrived and the crew cut the unfortunate Crawford free before picking up Pyke, who then discovered his comrade could not swim.

DATA TABLE

	Envelope capacity (cu.ft)	Overall length	Engines	Disposable lift	Top speed
Non-rigid airships					
Nulli Secundus	55,000	122ft	1 x 50hp Antoinette		16mph
Nulli Secundus II	56,000	122ft	1 x 50hp Antoinette		22mph
Baby	22,000	84ft	2 x 8hp Buchet, later 1 x 20–25hp REP		20mph
HMA 2 (*Willows IV*)	35,000	?	40hp Renault		25mph
HMA 3 (*Astra-Torres*)	230,000	248ft	2 x 200hp Chenu		51mph
HMA 4 (Parseval)	364,000	312ft	2 x 180hp Maybach		42mph
HMA 5 (V. Parseval)	364,000	304ft	2 x 240hp Renault		50mph
HMA 6 (V. Parseval)	364,000	304ft	2 x 180hp Wolseley/Maybach		42mph
HMA 7 (V. Parseval)	As HMA 6				
HMA 8 (Astra-Torres)	As HMA 3				
HMA 17 (*Beta II*)	50,000	108ft	1 x 45hp Clerget		35mph
HMA 18 (*Gamma II*)	101,000	169ft	2 x 45hp Iris		30mph
HMA 19 (*Delta*)	175,000	225ft	2 x 110hp White & Poppe		44mph
HMA 20 (*Eta*)	118,000	187ft	2 x 80hp Canton-Unné		42mph
SS BE2c	60,000	143ft 5in.	1 x 75hp Renault	0.64 tons	50mph
SS M. Farman	60,000/70,000	143ft 5in.	1 x 82hp Renault	0.6/0.8 tons	40mph
SS Armstrong Whitworth	70,000	143ft 5in.	1 x 100hp Green	0.7 tons	45mph
SS Pusher	70,000	143ft 5in.	1 x 75hp Rolls-Royce Hawk, later 1 x 100hp Green	0.6 tons	52mph
SS Zero	70,000	143ft 5in.	1 x 75hp Rolls-Royce Hawk	0.6 tons	53mph
SS Twin	100,000	165ft	2 x 75hp Rolls-Royce Hawk or 2 x 100hp Sunbeam	1 ton	57mph
C Class	170,000	195ft 6in.	2 x 150hp Sunbeam, later 1 x 220hp Renault & 1 x 100hp Berliet or Green	1.6 tons	52mph
C* Class	210,000	207ft (C*1– C*3) 217ft (C*4–C*10)	1 x 110hp Berliet & 1 x 220hp Renault (or 1 x 240hp Fiat)	1.8 tons	57mph
NS Class	360,000	260ft	2 x 250hp Rolls-Royce, later 2 x 240hp Fiat	3.8 tons	57mph
Semi-rigid airships					
SR.1	441,000	264ft	2 x 220hp Italia & 1 x 200hp SPA-6a	2.3 tons	51 mph
Rigid airships					
HMA 1r	664,000	512ft	2 x 180hp Wolseley	–	–
HMA 9r	846,000	526ft	2 x 180hp Wolseley & 1 x 240hp Maybach	3.8 tons	45mph
23 Class	942,000	535ft	4 x 250hp Rolls-Royce Eagle	6.5 tons	54mph
23X Class	990,000	539ft	4 x 300hp Rolls-Royce Eagle	8.5 tons	55mph
R.31 Class	1,500,000	615ft	6 x 300hp Rolls-Royce Eagle, later 5 x 300hp Rolls-Royce Eagle	16.5 tons 19.5 tons	70mph 65mph
R.33 Class	1,950,000	643ft	5 x 240hp Sunbeam Maori 4	26 tons	62mph
R.36	2,101,000	675ft	3 x 350hp Sunbeam Cossack & 2 x 260hp Maybach	16 tons	65mph
R.38	2,724,000	699ft	6 x 350hp Sunbeam Cossack	45.6 tons	71mph
R.80	1,200,000	535ft	4 x 230hp Wolseley-Maybach	15–18 tons	60–70mph
R.100	5,156,000	709ft	6 x 660hp Rolls-Royce Condor IIIB	57 tons	64mph
R.101	5,509,753	777ft	5 x 600hp Beardmore Tornado	49.3 tons	71mph

SELECT BIBLIOGRAPHY

Abbott, Patrick, *Airship*, Bath (1973)

Abbott, Patrick, *The British Airship at War 1914–1918*, Lavenham (1989)

Jackson, Robert, *Airships*, London (1971)

Mowthorpe, Ces, *Battlebags – British Airships of the First World War*, Stroud (1995)

Sinclair, J. A., *Airships in Peace and War*, London (1934)

Ventry, Lord & Kolesnik, Eugene M., *Airship Saga*, Poole (1982)

Vivian, E. Charles, *A History of Aeronautics*, London (1921)

Whale, George, *British Airships: Past, Present and Future*, London (1919)

Williams, Capt T. B., *Airship Pilot No.28*, London (1974)

An excellent source of information on British airships can be found at the website of the Airship Heritage Trust – **www.aht.ndirect.co.uk/**. As well as technical information, the website also gives access to contemporary newsreel footage of many of the airships highlighted in this book. In addition, the AHT publishes an excellent journal, *Dirigible*, three times a year.

The wreck of C.27 photographed from one of the attacking Hansa-Brandenburg seaplanes. A trawler skipper, watching from afar, reported: 'A cloud of smoke, very large and dense, hung in the sky for a long while'.

INDEX

Figures in **bold** refer to illustrations.

23 Class 26–28, **27**, C (28)
23X Class 28, **28**, 30

Air Battalion, Royal Engineers 5–6
Air Council 31
Airship Guarantee Company 36
Airships Ltd 16, 18, 19
Antoinette engines 6
armament 38
    bombs 20, 22, **23**, 24, 26, 40, E (40)
    depth charges 20, 39, 42
    Lewis guns 20, 24, 26, 39, E (40)
Armstrong Whitworth Ltd. 18, **18**, 19,
        27, 30, 31, 35
Army Aircraft Factory 6
Army airships 4, **4**, 5
    Baby and *Beta* 6–7, **7**
    Beta II 8, **8**, 16
    Clément-Bayard II 9–10, **10**
    Delta 10, **11**, 16
    Eta 11, **11**, 16
    Gamma and *Gamma II* 8, 8–9, **9**, 16
    Lebaudy Morning Post 9–10, **10**
    Nulli Secundus **5**, 6
    Nulli Secundus II 6, **6**
Army Balloon Equipment Store, Woolwich 5
Astra Company, Paris 8
Astra-Torres airship 12, 13, **13**, 16
Atlantic, crossing of **34**, D (32)
Avro seaplane fuselages 19

Baby and *Beta* 6–7, **7**
Bannerman, Maj **9**
Barrs, FltLt John E. E (40)
Beardmore 27, 30, 31, 35, 37
Berliet engines 19, 22
Beta II 8, **8**, 16
bombs **23**, 24, 26, 40, E (40)
Buchet engines 7

Canton-Unné engines **11**
Capper, Col J. E. 4, **4**, 6, 7, **7**, 8
Chenu engines 13
civil airships
    R.36: **34**, 34–35
    R.100: 36–37, **37**
    R101: 37–38, **38**
Clément-Bayard II 9–10, **10**
Clerget engines 8
Coastal (C) Class 19–21, 38–40, **40**,
        42–44, B (20)
Coastal Star (C*) Class 22, **22**, B (20)
Cody, S. F. 6
Coltson, FltSubLt C. S. 39
convoy system **40**
Crawford, W/T operator Frederick F (44)

Daily Mail 9
Delta 10, **11**, 16
depth charges 20, 39, 42
disposable lift 5
Dixon, FltLt J. F. 44

engines
    Antoinette engines 6
    Berliet engines 19, 22
    Buchet engines 7
    Canton-Unné engines **11**
    Chenu engines 13

Clerget engines 8
Fiat engines 22, 23
Green engines 7, 9, 19, 23
Iris engines 9, **9**
Maybach engines **14**, **26**, 34
Renault engines 14, 18, 19, 20, 22
Rolls-Royce Condor engines 37
Rolls-Royce Eagle engines 27, 30
Rolls-Royce Hawk engines 23, 24
Sunbeam engines 19, 24, 31, **35**
Tornado engines 37
White & Poppe engines 10
Wolseley engines 12
Wolseley-Maybach engines 26, 36
Eta 11, **11**, 16

Fiat engines 22, 23

Gamma and *Gamma II* 8, 8–9, **9**, 16
goldbeater's skin 6, 26, **26**
Green engines 7, 9, 19, 23

HMA No.1 12, **12**, 26
HMA No.9 26, **26**

Imperial Airship Scheme 36, **37**
Iris engines 9, **9**

Kinaldie **42**

Lebaudy Morning Post 9–10, **10**
Lewis guns 20, 22, 24, 26, 39, E (40)

M Class (semi-rigid airship) 25, **25**
Maitland, Maj E. M. **11**
Marne II **42**
Maurice Farman aircraft fuselages 19,
        19, 23
Maybach engines **14**, **26**, 34
Mayfly 12, **12**, 26
Monk, FltLt Errol F. 43, **43**
Montague, FltLt R. S. 39, 42–43
Moore, Capt T. P. 38–39
Morning Post 9–10

National Physical Laboratory (NPL) 31
Navy airships 15
    23 Class 26–28, **27**, C (28)
    23X Class 28, **28**, 30
    Astra-Torres airship 12, 13, **13**, 16
    Coastal (C) Class 19–21, 38–40, **40**,
        42–44, B (20)
    Coastal Star (C*) Class 22, **22**, B (20)
    HMA No.9 26, **26**
    North Sea (NS) Class 22–23, **23**,
        B (20)
    Parseval airship 13–14, **14**, 15–16
    R.31 Class **30**, 30–31, C (28)
    R.33 Class 31
    R.34: **34**, D (32)
    R.36: **34**, 34–35
    R.38: 35, **35**
    R.80: 35–36, **36**
    R.100: 36–37, **37**
    R.101: 37–38, **38**
    rigid airships 12, **12**, 26–38
    semi-rigid (SR) airships 25, **25**
    Submarine Scout Pusher (SSP) Class 23
    Submarine Scout (SS) Class **15**, 16, **18**,
        18–19, **19**, 43, **43**, A (16),
        F (44)

Submarine Scout Twin (SST) Class 24, **25**
    Submarine Scout Zero (SSZ) Class
        23–24, **24**, 42, **42**, 43, E (40)
    Willows No.4 12, **13**
non-rigid airships 5, 46
North Sea (NS) Class 22–23, **23**, B (20)
Nulli Secundus **5**, 6
Nulli Secundus II 6, **6**

Ouse, HMS **28**

Parseval airship 13–14, **14**, 15–16
Pullen, FltSubLt W. J. 42
Pyke, SubLt Cyril J. F (44)

R.31 Class **30**, 30–31, C (28)
R.33 Class 31
R.34: **34**, D (32)
R.36: **34**, 34–35
R.38: 35, **35**
R.80: 35–36, **36**
R.100: 36–37, **37**
R.101: 37–38, **38**
Renault engines 14, 18, 19, 20, 22
Richmond, LtCol Vincent 36
rigid airships 5, 12, 26–38, 46
Rigid Naval Airship I 12, **12**
Rolls-Royce Condor engines 37
Rolls-Royce Eagle engines 27, 30
Rolls-Royce Hawk engines 23, 24
Royal Airship Works (RAW) 35, 36
Royal Flying Corps 6, 14
Royal Naval Air Service (RNAS) 15

semi-rigid airships 5, 25, **25**, 46
Short Brothers 30, 35, C (28)
Spencer, Stanley 4
SR.1 airship 25, **25**
Star, HMS **28**
Submarine Scout Pusher (SSP) Class 23
Submarine Scout (SS) Class **15**, 16, **18**,
        18–19, **19**, 43, **43**, A (16), F (44)
Submarine Scout Twin (SST) Class 24, **25**
Submarine Scout Zero (SSZ) Class 23–24,
        24, 42, **42**, 43, E (40)
Sunbeam engines 19, 24, 31, **35**

Tattersall, W/T operator F. E. E (40)
Thompson, Lord 37
Times , *The* **27**
Tornado engines 37
Trevelyn, Engineer J. W. E (40)

UB-115 submarine **28**
useful lift 5

Vickers Sons & Maxim Ltd 12, 13–14,
        14, 26–27

Wallis, Barnes 36
weapons *see* armament
White & Poppe engines 10
Williams, T. B. A (16)
Willows, Ernest Thompson 4, **4**, 12
Willows No.1 4, **4**
Willows No.4 12, **13**
Wolseley engines 12
Wolseley-Maybach engines 26, 36
World War I (1914-18) 15–36, 38–45

Zeppelin airships 9, 12, 28, 34